SHEEP
ON THE FAMILY FARM

Chana Stiefel

Enslow Elementary

an imprint of

Enslow Publishers, Inc.

40 Industrial Road
Box 398
Berkeley Heights, NJ 07922
USA

http://www.enslow.com

CONTENTS

WORDS TO KNOW

breed—One type of animal in a group.

ewe—A female sheep.

fleece—Wool cut from a sheep.

graze—To feed on grass.

lamb—A baby sheep.

ram—A male sheep.

PARTS OF A SHEEP

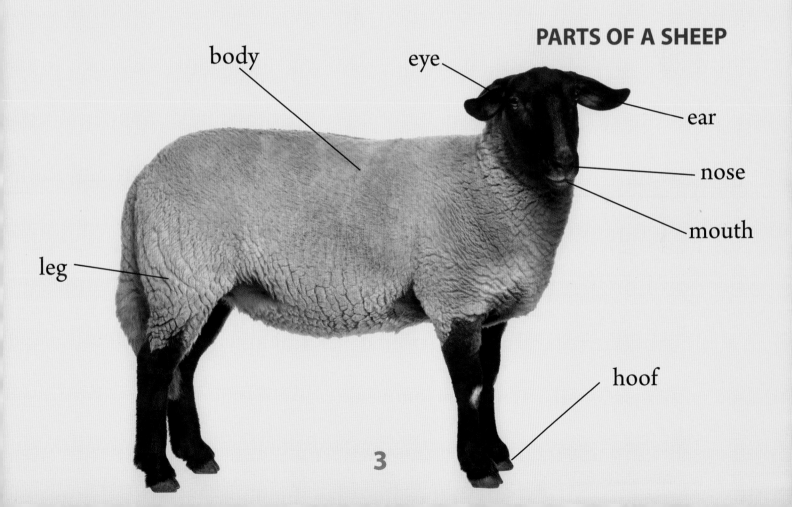

body

eye

ear

nose

mouth

leg

hoof

3

WONDERFUL
WOOL

4

Did you know that the wool from a single sheep could make as many as eight sweaters? To find out more fun facts about sheep on a family farm, read on!

"BAA, BAA!"

A group of sheep is called a flock.

Matt and Tara raise sheep on their family farm. They raise many other kinds of animals, too. Their children, Jack and Alice, help out with chores.

Matt and Tara raise five to ten sheep on their farm. Alice rides on Matt's shoulders when he checks on their flock.

Sheep need to eat grasses and plants to stay healthy. Matt and Tara keep their sheep away from horse nettle. This prickly plant can harm the sheep.

WHAT **SHEEP** EAT

Matt and Tara's sheep **graze** in the fields. They eat grass and weeds. They also like flowers. The sheep eat and chew all day.

9

WINTER DIET

It is lots of work to move the hay into the barn for the winter.

On cold winter days, Jack helps move the sheep into the barn. He feeds them hay. Hay is dry, cut grass. The sheep drink lots of water, too.

LITTLE LAMBS, BIG RAMS

A baby sheep is called a **lamb**. Its mother is called a **ewe** ("you"). Its father is a **ram**. Most types of rams have big horns that curl. Horns start to grow soon after a lamb is born. The horns grow all through the animal's life.

Rams use their horns when they fight with other rams. They might fight over a ewe.

ON THE
LOOKOUT

A hungry coyote is coming close to the flock! The sheep feel danger. They have sharp eyesight. Their ears perk up when they hear a sudden noise. They smell trouble. The sheep run away fast.

On many farms, a dog protects the sheep from coyotes, wolves, bears, and other animals.

HAVE YOU ANY WOOL?

On some farms, the farmers cut the sheep's wool. It is like a haircut. It does not hurt the sheep. The cut wool is called **fleece**. The fleece is cleaned and untangled. Then it is spun, or twisted, into threads of yarn. The yarn can be dyed many colors.

Yarn is knitted to make warm clothes and blankets. Some wool is used to weave carpets.

To make some cheese, the farmers can hang it in special cloth to dry.

FARM FRESH
FOOD

Some sheep are raised for milk.
The milk is made into cheese.
Matt and Tara's sheep are raised
for meat. The meat from an
adult sheep is called mutton.
If a sheep is less than a year old,
the meat is called lamb.

Sheep are grown for milk, cheese, and meat.

MANY KINDS OF SHEEP

Not all sheep are the same. There are more than 200 different **breeds**. One breed may be white. Other breeds are black, brown, gray, red, or spotted. Which do you like best?

Katahdin

Dorset

Jacob

Cotswold

Merino

Hampshire

LIFE CYCLE OF A SHEEP

1. A ewe gives birth to one, two, or three lambs at a time. A lamb is the size of a small dog. It weighs eight to ten pounds when it is born.

3. By one year, a lamb is an adult sheep. Sheep live for ten to twelve years.

2. Lambs drink their mother's milk. By one month, the lambs eat grass.

LEARN MORE

BOOKS

Macken, JoAnn Early. *Sheep*. Pleasantville, N.Y.: Weekly Reader, 2011.

Nelson, Robin. *Sheep*. Minneapolis, Minn.: Lerner Publications, 2009.

Schubert, Leda. *Feeding the Sheep*. New York: Farrar, Straus, and Giroux, 2010.

WEB SITES

Science Kids. *Animal Facts*. "Fun Sheep facts for Kids."
http://www.sciencekids.co.nz/sciencefacts/animals/sheep.html

Smithsonian National Zoological Park. *Kids' Farm*.
http://www.nationalzoo.si.edu/Animals/KidsFarm/IntheBarn

INDEX

Enslow Elementary, an imprint of Enslow Publishers, Inc.
Enslow Elementary® is a registered trademark of Enslow Publishers, Inc.

Copyright © 2013 by Chana Stiefel

All rights reserved.

No part of this book may be reproduced by any means
without the written permission of the publisher.

Library of Congress Cataloging-in-Publication Data

Stiefel, Chana, 1968-
    Sheep on the family farm / Chana Stiefel.
        p. cm. — (Animals on the family farm)
    Summary: "An introduction to an animal's life on a farm for early readers. Find out
what a sheep eats, where it lives, and what they are are like on a farm"—Provided by
publisher.
    Includes index.
    ISBN 978-0-7660-4209-4
    1. Sheep—Juvenile literature. I. Title. II. Series: Animals on the family farm.
    SF375.2.S74 2014
    636.3—dc23   2012028805

Future editions:
Paperback ISBN: 978-1-4644-0361-3
EPUB ISBN: 978-1-4645-1199-8
Single-User PDF ISBN: 978-1-4646-1199-5
Multi-User PDF ISBN: 978-0-7660-5831-6

Printed in China
012013 Leo Paper Group, Heshan City, Guangdong, China
10 9 8 7 6 5 4 3 2 1

To Our Readers: We have done our best to make sure all Internet Addresses in this
book were active and appropriate when we went to press. However, the author and the
publisher have no control over and assume no liability for the material available on
those Internet sites or on other Web sites they may link to. Any comments or
suggestions can be sent by e-mail to comments@enslow.com or to the address on the
back cover.

Photo Credits: Howling Wolf Farm, pp. 6, 7, 10; © iStockphoto.com/bernd Jonas, p. 9;
Photos.com: David Strydom, p. 20 (middle), Holly Kuchera, p. 15, Lakhesis, p. 19;
Shutterstock.com, p. 1, 2, 3, 4–5, 8, 11, 12, 13, 14, 16, 17, 18, 20 (left, right), 21, 22.

Cover Photo: John Spray/Photos.com

A note from Matt and Tara of Howling Wolf Farm: Howling Wolf Farm grows vital
food to feed individuals and families. Products include vegetables, dry beans and grains,
dairy, beef, eggs, chicken, lamb, and pork. We work in partnership with nature and
people to grow vibrant, abundant food. We farm with an intention of creating a farm
and food to bring health, vitality, and enjoyment to our complete beings and the land.
We focus on heirloom and open-pollinated varieties, heritage breeds, and wild foods.

Series Literacy Consultant:
Allan A. De Fina, Ph.D.
Past President of the New Jersey Reading Assoc.
Dean of the College of Education
New Jersey City University
Jersey City, NJ

Series Science Consultant:
Dana Palmer
Sr. Extension Associate/4-H Youth Outreach
Department of Animal Science
Cornell University
Ithaca, NY